365 More Ways to say "I Love You"

BY JANI GARDNER

HAWTHORN BOOKS, INC.

PUBLISHERS   NEW YORK

For my own continuing Chase

January

Invite him to a New Year's Day soirée *chez vous* and lose the list of other invitees. Then forget all those good resolutions you made.

Black lace "smalls" and net stockings never did a French maid any harm.

Check all the buttons on all his suits. There's bound to be one or two missing, and he probably hates to ask.

Reread *Lady Chatterley* and some of those other "prurient" classics. A good idea is never out of date.

Call up the people you didn't see on New Year's Day and invite them to a "week later party." Explain that "he" was the person you most wanted to spend that day with and let him hear you.

Sneak out at midnight and get him three king-sized cheeseburgers at McDonald's to celebrate the Feast of the Three Kings.

Take a bubble bath together. Tub too small? So much the better.

Explore and massage his feet while he watches TV.

Next time he suggests an evening walk, wear your fur coat and nothing else. No one else will guess, but you'll blow his mind.

Greet him at the front door with a "Jump Up and Kiss Me." It's a specialty of the Buccaneer Hotel in St. Croix, Virgin Islands. Mix up the following:

    1 ounce Galliano
    1 ounce pineapple juice
    1 ounce Barbados rum
    ¼ ounce apricot-flavored brandy
    1 egg white or ½ ounce Frothy

Add crushed ice and put in blender for about 60 seconds. Serve in an enormous brandy snifter.

Resolve to clear off a section in the already too cluttered hall closet for his so very losable winter gear—gloves, mufflers, ice skates.

Get him a set of body paints and offer your services as a model.

Throw away all your girdles.

Paint his name on a long silk scarf the way chic designers sign their names to their scarves, buttons, and so on.

Ask him if he'd like to start the year off right by joining Smoke Stoppers. Write to their headquarters at 519 West 57th Street, New York City, for further data. If he does decide to quit, keep yourself pretty: You'll probably be the substitute vice.

Take pictures of him. Seems like he always gets stuck taking photographs of you. Tuck one in your nightie drawer. He'll secretly love it.

Call Pan Am and reserve seats for the earliest convenient moon flight. Might be a fun way to celebrate your fiftieth anniversary.

Remember that old one: Cover me with chocolate and lick me all over—I like a sundae kind of love? Might try it next time life seems a bit boring.

Explore him for places you may have missed.

Tell him you like him best in his naked state on Inauguration Day. And on every other day, too.

Make up a special I Love You key chain for him. Work in any media you wish: cardboard, lucite, plastic. If it turns out to be too spectacular, he can use it for his locker key.

Light a candle by his bed tonight.

Leave a note in his shaving kit asking what color nightie he would like to see you in when next you meet.

Get him to the church or synagogue of his choice on time some Sunday. It might be a whole new experience.

Rub noses in the morning before he gets up.

Move the record player to the bedroom and use it.

Put a note inside the phone book asking: "How did we ever find each other?"

Sprint about the house in shape-up sandals when he's not around. He'll notice someday when you're cavorting on the beach.

Let him know that you think he's the best lover in the world, that the words "virile" and "manly" went undefined before he came along.

Wear a snippet of his hair in a golden locket around your neck. This is very Victorian and very romantic.

Walk him to work one morning. Well, to the subway, train, bus, car. And kiss. A lot.

February

Prepare a special dinner in celebration of last night's snow-fall. Make everything white, starting with cream soup and ending with angel cake with marshmallow topping.

Light up your nest exclusively with candles in honor of Candlemas. But keep in mind the Great Blackout birth statistics. Candles are not so innocent as they look.

On Groundhog Day, wake him up at the crack of dawn to see if he's crabby. If he is, get him up at the usual hour. If not, let him sleep a little longer.

Take belly-dance classes or learn to strip like Gypsy or brush up on your tap dancing. Do whatever turns him on. There are kinds and kinds of adult ed.

Get a plaque for the inside of his car saying: "This car belongs to ———, whom I love."

Clear out a corner of the freezer and freeze a batch of snow-balls for summer fun.

Try doing without the assistance of a bra—at least at home. Very sexy, this.

Get him a "what-did-you-bring-me" present when you go out on errands.

Put some Cornhuskers Lotion in his workshop for these cold days. It's one of the only really masculine ones around.

Learn how to whisper in his ear with your mouth open.

Learn how to whisper in his ear with your mouth shut.

Suggest he grow a beard or moustache in honor of the bearded President Lincoln's birthday.

Seduce *him* for a change. Greet him at the door in a sheer negligee and a come-hither look. He'll take over from there.

For Valentine's Day send for a very special red leather book from the Little Rock Library Bindery, Highway 10, Little Rock, Arkansas. They'll title the book anything you want. The pages are blank, so pen in your own special thoughts about him.

Invite him to take you to a hamburger stand. They're not crowded in February, and besides, they're cheap and fun. Men love to take us out, but they hate to spend money.

Dig through his baby pictures and frame some in look-what-I-found-at-the-antique-shop frames. If you can get away with it, put the famous bear-rug one on your bedside table.

Tell him he's the best "live-in" you've ever had.

Tell his fortune from tarot cards. Make sure it's a good one, featuring a beautiful lady who just happens to look like you.

Let him mess up your clean kitchen cooking his special gourmet thing. He'll get more fun out of it than you will work.

Wrap up a gift certificate saying "Good for anything you ever want from me. Happy Today. I Love You." Don't forget the bow. You'll have as much fun when he collects as he will!

Pencil on the fish-fry notice you got in the mail that you'd "flounder through life without him."

Go willingly to his niece's piano recital. It can't be that bad. Well, all right, it can. But you'll be holding his hand, so who cares?

Mix him up some Glühwein, which is what you two would be drinking if you were at a resort skiing right now. Bring the following ingredients to a boil:

    2 cups red wine
    2 pieces lemon rind
    8 cloves
    2 pieces cinnamon
    ⅔ cup sugar or to taste

Strain and serve piping hot.

In the middle of a party say, "I think we should go home and make love," and do it.

Lean over and open the car door for him when he's locked out. It's a little thing, but it saves him a step and shows you love him.

Snuggle up to him while watching the sad-ending movie. The happy-ending movie. The TV.

Conduct a careful study of his erogenous zones. And make use of your knowledge!

Meet him at the breakfast table in a mask (and nothing else) in honor of Mardi Gras.

March

Don't notice when he marches in like a lion after work. You would too if your secretary quit at 9:30, *before* the coffee break.

Tell him you plan to change the shape of things as you stand on a scale in front of the refrigerator.

Keep masses of fresh-cut flowers in the bedroom at all times. This is really worth the extra pennies—well, all right, quarters.

Spend the evening sketching each other in the nude. Forget that you can't draw a straight line. This isn't really for improving your *artistic* talent.

If you're planning a trip to La Belle France, save a little extra to light up some of the famous monuments of the City of Light. The Eiffel Tower lights up for $55, the Arc de Triomphe for $26.50, and the Louvre for $14.30.

Make him a special plate of silver-dollar pancakes for his breakfast-in-bed treat. It'll put him in the mood for an after-breakfast-in-bed treat.

Stash a windproof lighter in his jacket pocket.

Send him a postcard inviting him to see a thriller at the drive-in.

Get a pet gerbil from the local animal store. Actually, a pair would be better. They are adorable, and he won't even have to walk them.

Hide in the closet naked when you know he's going to hang up his tie.

Sing "Oh, no, you can't take that away from me" when he gets up early in the morning to go to work.

Pin a carnation in his lapel unbeknownst to him. Carnations are the special flower for March.

Put a note in his shorts saying that the pleasures of a temporary affair are nothing like the pleasures of living with him.

Start breakfast with an icy split of champagne.

Dig into your recipe books for delightful pastry goodies. He'll love you for it, and besides, it makes the whole house smell homey.

Stop being a whirlwind when he's in a relaxing mood. The poor man needs to rest after a long day at work. Let him get up his strength for later in the evening when he'll need it.

On St. Patrick's Day, parade around the bedroom in a small green towel.

Pin a note with Christina Rossetti's lines so he'll find it when he comes home:

> My heart is like a rainbow shell
> That paddles in a halcyon sea:
> My heart is gladder than all these,
> Because my love is come to me.

Have a brass door plaque made up which reads: "———— slept here." Put it above your bed.

If March winds and rains cause the flu bug to bite at your house, make sure there are lots of super reading materials around. And serve all meals on a different tray arrangement. Use everything from doilies to ice-cream-filled tiny flower-pots. And forget the thermometer. You know it's just a bug.

Put some Tootsie Rolls in his cuff-link box.

Scribble a note inside his passport case in case he goes somewhere sometime. You can do better than "Remember me when far away."

Ask him if he'd like to join the Society for Creative Anachronism so you could spend time sitting around holding hands, singing madrigals, dancing gaillards, and watching jousters at their game while you sip ale and honey. He'll feel you look upon him as a knight in shining armor.

See that he laughs at least twice a day.

Every once and a while—without telling him—change the bulbs in the bedroom lamps to sexy red or soft lavender.

Wait another month to ask him to clean out the garage. In fact, why not just hire one of the neighborhood kids to do it for him?

Stick a "Happy Thursday" pennant on his plate of sausages. (If it's Thursday, dummy.)

Ask him furtively, "When will I see you again?" as he leaves for work.

Dab a tiny drop of your perfume on his necktie. He'll think of you all day and wonder why.

Print this Irish Blessing on a bookmark for him. Maybe you can even learn to print with an osmiroid pen.
> May the road rise to meet you.
> May the wind be always at your back.
> May the sun shine warm upon your face,
> The rain fall soft upon your fields.
> And until we meet again, may God
> Hold you in the palm of His hand.

Shell a one-pound bag of pistachio nuts just for him.

April

Play rub-a-dub-dub when he comes out of the tub.

Call his office to tell him he was rejected by the Ugly Modeling Agency of London. It's an agency where really ugly people, warts and all, can make six guineas ($15) per hour.

Take care of him when he's hung over. It's when he needs you most. But do it ver-r-y quietly.

Stash some peanuts in the glove compartment for a traffic-jam diversion.

Wake him up telling him you can't possibly imagine how April could be the cruelest month, especially now that you've discovered him.

Take a hop around your local airport in a teeny plane to celebrate the greening of the grasses. You can see best from on top.

Color Easter eggs together. Bet you haven't done that in a long time.

Invest in a set of black satin sheets, just for fun.

Exercise every day. A limber body enhances love-making. (Love-making enhances a limber body.)

Name an Arbor Day tree and have a permanent marker made up for it: "Here stands ———, which we planted together on ———."

Trace his front teeth with your finger.

Scrawl both your initials on the wall of a deserving restroom in some roadside hideaway. And tell him.

Offer to lick the envelope enclosing the income tax.

Arrange for a hearse to pick him up for his trip to the income-tax office.

Whip up a set of banana splits to celebrate your ——th day together.

Kiss like the movie stars do.

Get a magician to pull a love note out of his hat when he says "Abracadabra" at the night club you and your guy plan to attend.

Invite him to a pajama party. Just you two.

Shoot marbles in bed.

Whisper something, anything, in his ear. Women don't seem to do this much anymore, but it can be very sexy.

Burn incense at the foot of the bed.

Ask him to hang a rubber tire from a strong tree for a swing the way they did in Aprils long ago. Wear a full skirt, à la Marilyn Monroe, that the wind can toss up when he pushes you on the swing.

Give credit to Shakespeare, whose birthday is in April, and use his line "How many million Aprils came before I ever knew." Add to these some words that only you and your love will understand.

Send him a thank-you note thanking him for him.

Send his mother a thank-you note thanking her for him.

Tell him you'll wear your hair in an Afro if he finds it aphro.

Embroider a pillow in his study with the words "What *nice* can I do for you today?"

Get him some sexy men's underwear.

Serve dinner in bed.

Hide an egg in his shoe near the bed.

May

Put a notebook beside your bed for those midnight love notes you dream up.

Invite him by mail to build sand castles by the sea with you.

Send his mother roses on his birthday.

Send his father a cigar on his birthday.

Consult your library's aphrodisiac section and make a list of some of those potent potions. Try them out on your man and see what happens.

If ear-nibbling doesn't turn him on, try nose-nibbling. There's a whole underground cult of nose-nibblers and nose-nibblees.

Call him up at the office to ask him the name of that body-contact game you were learning last night.

Ask him to go looking for an in-town *pied-à-terre* kind of place with you. Tell him you want just a room, no kitchen, and a bed.

At dinner say, "Two more hours . . ."

Turn down the lights, put on some soft and sexy music, and dance together. Nude.

Touch him.

Be available. If you're cooking dinner, reading a mystery, balancing a checkbook—forget it! Burned roasts, unsolved murders, and bounced checks are as nothing when it comes to keeping your man happy.

Tape a photo of you two inside the lid of his briefcase.

Get up at dawn and go for an early moring dip *au naturel*. Then pick wild strawberries for breakfast.

Plant an "I Love You" note in the window of a store that's for lease. Beseech the landlord. They let girls do anything if they're persuaded.

Play Strip Scrabble: Any word worth under 15 points means you must forfeit an article of clothing.

Laugh at his jokes even if you're tired.

Invite him to see a re-run of anything on TV tonight.

Read out loud to him all the sexy bits in your current novel.

Put a yo-yo in his lunch box. Don't forget the sandwiches.

On Derby Day, have a special Finnish celebration: a groaning buffet called *voileipiapoyta*. A sample one might feature a meat and rice casserole, peas, baked carrot custard, Finnish meat balls, cold cuts, and herring salad. Deck the table out with a green cloth and a simulated racetrack made out of white tape and complete with finish line. Remember to start off with the celebrated Kentucky Mint Juleps. After all this work, he'll know *you* love him—even if his horse lost.

Send him a letter at the office suggesting he bring the boss home for dinner. Plan a special spur-of-the-moment meal in case he takes you up on it in the near future.

Put a special note inside one of his hub caps. The day he finds it, he'll love you all over the map.

Try not to be bull-headed in an argument with your guy. Just because May has the bull for a sign is no reason for you to show it.

Robert Browning talks about "May's warm, slow, yellow moonlit summer nights." You should, too. So invite him on a tour of the neighborhood. A lot has happened since the time of the snow shovel.

Plant a pot of pansies to take to his office.

Order a hammock *à deux* for summer evening happenings.

Plant bright-colored marigolds in the flower boxes around the outside windows. And don't ask him to help.

Have a bacchanalian dinner: Everything must be eaten with the hands, à la that famous scene in *Tom Jones;* gallons of wine are quaffed; and your own private orgy must go on before, during, and after the fete.

Ask him if a fish pond in the back yard would make him happy. If it would, have one built. If it wouldn't, settle for a goldfish in a bowl.

Begin calling things "ours." Don Quixote had a thing about "those two fatal words, Mine and Thine." And for once, he knew what he was talking about.

June

Post a note to him at the office asking, "And what is so rare as a day in June?" as did James Russell Lowell. Then suggest that he take the afternoon off and come play with you.

Sing the "Battle Hymn of the Republic" when he rises in honor of the birthday of Jefferson Davis early in June. And give him grapes (but not of wrath) for breakfast.

Paste a tiny black tattoo of a butterfly on your left breast. Let him discover it.

Send him off to work with a fresh package of figs in his briefcase.

Cut a perky bunch of posies for the bathroom, that usually so-neglected room.

Prepare everything for the cookout ahead of time so he need only come on out and enjoy the fun. Most fellas would just as soon eat in as go to all the trouble of setting up outside.

Send him a bill for "services rendered." Don't itemize it.

Buy a one-minute spot on the FM station he listens to and expound his virtues—or at least one minute's worth of them.

Embroider "I Love You" inside his swim trunks.

Make him a bug jug for catching lightning bugs. Then carry on the rest of your night's activities by the light of only these little creatures. Romantic!

Give him some giant bath towels in vivid colors for Father's Day. He is maybe tired of always sharing his with you.

Run hand in hand through a warm rain storm like you did when you first met.

Make sure he's got a table for his drinks, glasses, etc. (mostly etc.) near his hammock or favorite outdoor spot. It's a loving gal who helps to organize her guy.

Make some patriotic pillows for his hammock from white, red, and blue striped and starred fabric. Trail a "Happy Flag Day" banner over the whole deal.

Scout through your old costume jewelry for a particularly lurid bauble. Fashion it into a navel jewel and model it for your man. Might even throw in a few steps of the Dance of the Seven Veils—*sans* veils, of course.

Set a rose out with his morning paper.

Whisper "I love you" when he has a seashell to his ear.

Shake up a frosty pitcher of sangría to greet him after his trek home in the heat. Mix together:

    1 quart dry red wine
    2 cups soda water
    ⅔ cup granulated sugar
    1 peach, sliced
    1 lemon, sliced
    1 orange, sliced
    1 lime, sliced
    1 banana, sliced
    1 apple, sliced
    1 tablespoon brandy, not sliced
Stir in ice and serve in huge glass mugs.

Plant some grape-ivy in an old white birdcage and hang it in his favorite room. Grape-ivy trails all over the place and looks very romantic.

Write "I Love You" in red crayon on the soles of his tennis shoes. He'll see it when he unpacks in the locker room.

Foil the rumor about June bustin' out all over and save your bikini for August. There's still time to drop some pounds.

Put some extra sun-screen lotion in the glove compartment for trafficky top-down days.

Save up grocery money to rent a houseboat for a weekend and rechristen it *Honeymoon II.*

Nuzzle the inside of his knee.

Agree to go along on the fishing trip. I'm sure he'll bait all the hooks and all you'll have to do to earn your keep is rise at daybreak and grill those fresh fish for breakfast. That's all?

Lie together on a hill in the park and play cloud games. Zero in on a cloud and decide what it looks like. Think sexy.

Run to him when it lightnings and thunders. If it's night and you're not already in the same bed, get there.

Don't ask who's on the phone.

Celebrate Kamehameha Day. They do in Hawaii, but I don't know why.

Try greeting him at the door with slippers, pipe, newspaper, and martini. This one's so old you've probably never even tried it.

July

Gather together those battered old boxes of childhood games—Monopoly, Parchesi, Dominoes—and challenge him to a Sunday-morning gamefest in bed.

Ask the Government Supply Office where to get sunglasses that alter their color to suit the intensity of the sun's light. Get some to salvage your man's eyes from the brightness of July.

Get him to bed early for the blast tomorrow. Even if you haven't planned one, there's always somebody who brings in a crowd.

Start the Fourth of July festivities with Stone Fences on red, white, and blue striped cloths. Stone Fences are a colonial beverage, sometimes called Stonewalls, made with bourbon, cider, and applejack. I don't like to talk about people, but maybe the President had something to do with it.

Circle a torrid passage in a pornograph and inscribe it, "They copied."

On his birthday, wrap your naked self up in glittery tinfoil and tie a red satin bow round your middle (you may need the help of a friend for this one). Without doubt, this will be the package he opens first.

Make him a string of love beads with your own tiny hands.

Learn to purr, soft and throaty, like a cat when he scratches your back.

Tell him his headmistress is more than satisfied with his progress.

Read and heed the ads about not wearing curlers to bed or anywhere, for that matter, outside your own dressing chamber.

Stop crabbing about the heat and serve him a zesty crabmeat salad as an hors d'oeuvre when he comes home. You already know the crab is July's sign.

Get him some ear stopples in case somebody in the neighborhood likes the baseball game too loud when he's having a lazy afternoon nap.

Deposit a cookbook on his desk with a note asking for suggestions for tonight's dinner. It'll probably come back saying "Oh, anything," but you've learned how to handle that. It may, however, say "love" on it somewhere.

On Bastille Day, devote yourself to thinking up new ways to storm his defenses.

Serve him breakfast outside in the sunshine. Slather whipped cream over puffy waffles and top with strawberries. He'll think about you all the way to work.

Make an "I Love You" stencil (inside out), tape it on your tummy or back, and roast in the sun for about two hours. You'll be the toast of the beach when you peel it off.

Watch him shave this morning—very masculine. Queen Vicky plagued Albert in this fashion every morning of their long and reputedly happy life together.

Wake him up to one of his favorite records, set up by you the night before.

Send him a postcard saying, "I'm glad you're here" a couple days before you leave for your vacation. Address it to your chosen vacation spot.

Tuck this little note as a bookmark in the book he's currently reading:

> You are my poem then, for in my heart
> Lovelier than a sonnet, you made rhyme
> And I had memorized you unaware.

If he asks, it was written by Sir Thomas Browne. If he doesn't, who needs to tell?

Write up a menu for dinner. In the dessert section, put your name. You might call yourself Flaming So-and-So. He'll get the message.

Paint his name in the multicolored sections of the family beach ball.

Tell him that your Theory of Relativity is that relatives aren't so bad—really—in small doses and, yes, it would be fun to have his over for a cookout.

Comb his hair and scratch the back of his neck while singing his favorite lullaby.

Get a set of Boule balls from Abercrombie & Fitch and learn how.

Introduce yourself and start your acquaintance all over again. Nothing quite equals the mystery and anticipation of the first time.

Tell him that your life with him has been one serendipitous experience after another. If he doesn't know what it means, look it up for him.

Call him to come see a rainbow.

Get some of that sexy new breast make-up and experiment. Beauty doesn't stop at the neck, remember.

Run your tongue down the inside of his arm.

Greet him at the door as if he had been gone for many a year.

August

In England they celebrate Lammas Day, the festival of the wheat harvest, so turn on the air conditioner and bake him some real bread.

Establish an annual "You and Me Day," since August contains no national U.S. holidays. That means the two of you do whatever you please all day. And you know what that means!

Have his best character traits set in type at the local print shop. With his name at the top and a handsome frame, he'll love it.

When was the last time *you* sent *him* flowers?

Put away your pennies for a rainy day. When it comes, you take *him* out to dinner.

Wear his high-school ring on a chain around your neck. Don't bother to wear anything else.

Loll about the front porch together with frozen hot chocolate:

>   3 unsweetened chocolate squares
>   ¼ cup dark corn syrup
>   ⅓ cup sugar
>   3 cups milk
>   2 teaspoons vanilla
>   whipped topping
>   chocolate shavings

Combine chocolate squares, sugar, and corn syrup in a saucepan. Cook and stir until blended. Then add 3 cups milk, a teeny bit at a time, stirring after each addition until smooth. Add vanilla and remove from heat. Put into a 9-inch-square pan or the equivalent in another shape. Freeze for 1⅓ to 2 hours. Should freeze up to 1 inch from edge. When ready to drink, stir to blend. Serve in chilled glasses. Better have a spoon and straw, too. Top with whipped topping and chocolate shavings. Serves 4. Don't tell him about the calories. He doesn't want to hear.

Cut out the funnies from the stacks of unread newspapers you find when you return from your vacation. Otherwise, he'll miss all the Pogo and Peanuts and etc.'s tongues-in-cheek.

Create a special cabinet for his fishing lures. Take a standard Coca-Cola case, the kind with 24 slots, and paint it up bright. Fill each slot with a small baby-food jar whose lid has been painted a fun color, too. Tell him that the jars are for the lures and bait, if he can't figure it out. But don't be depressed if he thanks you kindly and then continues to dump his lures in his old tackle box. Men are like that.

Use his swim trunks for the flag on a sand castle you two build on the beach. Better make it a very private beach!

Get a pet turtle and name it after him.

Ask one of your artistic friends (Come now! Everyone has an artistic friend.) to paint (or charcoal, watercolor, etc.) his portrait.

Brush his teeth.

Meet him at the steamy train with an icy towel soaked in Brut.

In a lush vegetable store, tell him what fun he would be in the Garden of Eden.

Investigate him for places you've never kissed and repair the oversight.

When a friend calls, tell him it's the City Council answering your query about whether you can name a street after him.

Feed him mangoes and papayas held by your own delicate fingers.

Have a picture of him in the surf blown up into poster size at the local poster shop. Tell him that Muscle Beach should only know what it's missing.

Send him an ad for a torrid movie you'd like to see with him.

Remember those snowballs you froze last winter? Now's the perfect time to make use of them.

If your hair is long and luxurious (lucky girl!), ask him to brush it for you—like the heroines of bygone days.

Show him the ad in the paper that says: "Husband wanted —to take his charming wife to dinner." He should take the hint and have a nice time.

Keep quiet while he watches the news on TV.

Start a present drawer so Christmas gifts for him won't be such a last-minute puzzle.

Treat his minutes like an ounce of Joy.

Read him a bedtime story. Maybe from the *Kama Sutra?*

Read yourself Dr. Otto's *More Joy in Your Marriage* and don't say I didn't tell you.

Explain his problems to a health-food store manager and see what he suggests. Make sure it tastes good, whatever it is.

Call his mother on her birthday.

Spend an evening pretending that you're Jean Harlow and he's Clark Gable.

September

On Labor Day, bring him breakfast in bed and try to serve him lunch there, too.

When you're all alone with him, don't be shy or (heaven forbid!) inhibited. Be free to say and do anything you think might give him pleasure.

Kowtow to his late-in-the-season sunburn. Make love in a cool shower.

Rent a motorcycle for the day and go somewhere far away. Tell him that you, like Mae West, like an easy rider.

Get him a bundle of bath toys. Men never outgrow rubber ducks that go quack!

As a special gift, wash and wax the car for him. It will probably be the last time you get to wear your bikini this year, anyway.

Tickle his tummy with your fresh-washed hair.

Put some Callard and Bowser's butterscotch candies in his pockets. They're a handy sweet, and for some reason men love the taste of butterscotch.

Read aloud to him from your sexy novel while he changes yet another tire.

Surprise him with a *New York Times* front page from the date of his birth. Write to The New York Times Front Page, Box 557, New York, N.Y. 10036. It costs $1.50. You might want to get one to commemorate your anniversary or another special day. When days are special, who knows or remembers what's happening in the rest of the world?

Trust him completely. That's a lot of what love is all about.

Embroider "I Love You" on his tennis-racket cover.

Get him teed off early at the golf course. Men love getting at things early.

Start a charm bracelet of special places and things he's done with you.

Tell him there are anti-trust laws about lovers being jealous and you're trying hard to heed the law, but it's very difficult because you know there's not a girl in the world who could resist him.

Become a franchise welcomer and take him along to greet the new management every time a new franchise outfit opens up in your town. If nothing else, you'll get lots of free balloons.

On American Indian Day spend the night with him in a tent in the back yard. A blanket thrown over the clothesline will do. And remember—one sleeping bag!

Tackle him.

Con him into a round or two of miniature golf. Lose gracefully.

Never let the sun set on your anger. I'd love to pass that off as my own sage saying, but it's not. Anyway, do what it says, and you'll both wake up happy each morning.

Celebrate the last lush summer mornings by serving him tropical fruit in bed. Wear a Tahitian sarong and a bare bosom.

After another one of those gorgeous bubble baths *à deux*, nibble his toes.

Bake him a homemade peach pie and with a fork poke his name in the top crust.

Compose a romantic haiku for him to treasure.

Remember sunsets.

Forget how to say "What did you say?" Always try to listen hard the first time he says something. That business about him feeling ten-feet tall has to do with your making him think his every word is a gem.

Get him a locker combination spelling I-L-O-V-E-Y-O-U.

Circumnavigate a work-filled Saturday with a delightful country ride.

Stroke him all over with a soft, plumey feather. This will either put him to sleep or the opposite. Plug for the opposite.

Go to an "-in." That's love-in, wine-in, fly-in, and so on. People are into everything these days.

October

I.Sherman

Take him a candy apple while he's raking leaves. Maybe it'll make him forget you didn't offer to help him with them.

Read *The Magic of Walking* by Sussman and Goode and relay the data into action with your guy. You can discover a lot of good things on a walk—maybe even each other.

Notice the simple, everyday things he does for you. And let him know you notice.

Never ask "How much do you love me?"

Request a local disc jockey to play a record for him. Somebody he knows is bound to be listening, so you know he'll hear about it.

Make your own copy of the Robert Indiana "Love" poster in miniature and stash it under his pillow.

Suggest he have a beer with the boys tonight, since you've got some something to catch up on. Make up that "something."

Write to the head of the Institute of Linguistics at the Center for Advanced Study in Behavioral Sciences in Stanford, California, if you want to find out how to say "I love you" in Usarufa, White Tai, Terena, Amuesha, or Mazatec. Show the letter to your man. He'll think you're awfully inquisitive. But cute.

Prepare hot curried peaches to warm him up before the game.

1 can of cling peaches, the 1-pound-14-ounce kind
3 tablespoons butter or margarine
¼ cup brown sugar, packed firmly
½ teaspoon curry powder

Place peaches, open side up, in a glass baking dish. Daub with butter and sprinkle with a mixture of the sugar and curry. Bake ten minutes. Sugar should brown lightly. Serves six, or you two several times.

Get him a magazine subscription to match a hobby, e.g., *Oceans* or *Psychology Today*. More are on the market every day.

Send him a pressed flower to remind him of your radiant summer days together and include Mark Twain's thought "Grief can take care of itself, but to get the full value of a joy you must have somebody to divide it with."

On Columbus Day decide your bed's a raft. Hold on to him tightly to stay afloat. And don't forget mouth-to-mouth resuscitation if the sea gets rough.

Garnish his umbrella with a note commenting that he always makes the sun shine through.

Bring him some banana bread at midnight. (It's in your cookbook under "B.")

Give him an old-fashioned alcohol rub with a new twist—scotch (or vodka or gin or etc.) instead of that nasty-smelling hospital stuff. Run your tongue up his spine as a grand finale for both of you.

Prepare a warm and lemony footbath for him after a hard day's work.

Send him an invitation to spend a weekend in a camper with you. If he says the weather's not right, send him a poem note containing Helen Hunt Jackson's lines:

> O suns and skies and clouds of June,
> And flowers of June together,
> Ye cannot rival for one hour
> October's bright blue weather.

So there.

Put a note in his sock saying that you're having trouble handling your ecstasy quotient with him.

Build the first roaring fire of the season in your fireplace tonight and pop popcorn.

If you have a lot of house to clean, investigate the services of a cleaning woman. Think of it not as self-indulgence but as a gift to him. After all, the last thing he wants to see in the evening is an exhausted lady with housemaid's knee.

Make home movies—for your strictly private viewing.

Search for a myna bird that belonged to a little ol' lady from Pasadena and teach it to repeat "I love you" every morning.

Discover eye-kissing. Don't let anyone tell you it's inactive.

Get him some ginger drops for his plaid-shirt pocket.

Put a touch of "your" perfume on all the light bulbs in the house. The heat will spread the scent all over and drive your man wild.

Make a scrapbook of your life together: letters, photos, matchbooks, champagne corks, whatever. Look through it whenever you feel a little unappreciated.

Sit up and talk all night when there's a full moon.

Carve an imaginative Halloween pumpkin together. Then wash and toast and salt the pumpkin seeds for a TV snack.

Stir up some Witches' Brew. The Strega people who supply the 80-proof stuff say that the two people who drink it are united by a love that lasts forever. To mix the magic brew, shake or blend in a blender:

  ¾ ounce Strega
  ½ ounce gin
  1 ounce orange juice
  ¼ ounce lemon juice

Pour over ice cubes into a miniature cauldron or old-fashioned glass. They say it's a bewitching experience!

Make love by the light of your jack-o'-lantern.

Give him a generous sampling of your own special tricks and treats tonight.

November

Put a love note in the cord of wood outside. Use crayon so it doesn't get rained away.

Make a pine-cone centerpiece for his dresser.

Introduce him to some exotic cheeses and wines. And anything else exotic that occurs to you.

On an icy morning, turn the shower on to hot for a few minutes to warm up the bathroom for him.

Get him a piggy bank for atop his dresser so he doesn't get bugged by the loose change.

Stash a love note in the fresh towels stacked near the shower.

Get ready for next year's batch of I Love You's by sending in for "Chase's Calendar of Annual Events." It's full of special occasions for every day so you can dream up celebrations for your lover. Send $3 to Apple Tree Press, Box 1012, Flint Michigan.

It may sound quaint, but there's really nothing like a glowingly warm hot-water bottle in the bottom of the bed on frosty nights to greet cold toes.

Pack him a thermos of strong, hot coffee for that morning traffic jam.

Chase November gloom with stacks of romantic records on repeat.

On Armistice Day, patch up the slightest quarrel you might have had with a Western Union I-Didn't-Mean-It-Gram.

Shower the house with vivid paper flowers to make up for the fresh ones that are no more (at least not in our price bracket).

Have a lot of mirrors in the bedroom.

Make up bawdy limericks.

Send him a mash note.

Animate your love in a flashing light bulb from Takashi-maya at 509 Fifth Avenue in New York City. It blinks "I Love You."

Stop nagging him to grow sideburns or to cut them if he's got them.

Nibble his ear while he's buckling his belt.

Have his handwriting analyzed.

Borrow a nursing student's handbook on massage. And while you're at it, remember that the back isn't the only place that likes a good massage.

Renew his subscription to *Playboy*.

Draw up a phony ballot for Election Day and fill his name in on all the lines.

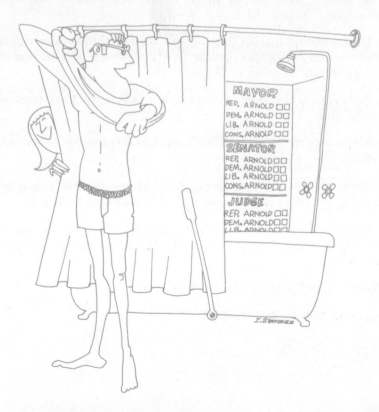

Invite him to a midnight candlelight supper. Wear black velvet and vamp him.

Climb into the shower with him.

If your hair is long and lovely, ask him to brush it for you. (You can brush his if it is long and lovely, too.)

Go to a drive-in and leave the windshield wipers on, lest there be any doubt.

See how much billboard advertising costs. I know a woman in Washington who rented a billboard to say "Happy Birthday!"

Learn Morse code for "I love you" and tap it out on the small of his back.

Tape a special note on the bathroom mirror on Thanksgiving Day thanking him for your wonderful life together. Add four lines from Charles Stuart Calverley:
> When the forest nymphs are beading
> Fern and flower with silvery dew
> My infallible proceeding
> Is to wake, and think of you.

Make love on a fur rug in front of the fireplace on a cold, dark night .

December

Z. Sherman

Put a balloon in his lunch box. Tell him to blow it up and put his Christmas list inside. You can launch it after he comes home and hope it makes it to the North Pole.

On a cold, cold morning, pop his stiff and icy shirt into a warm oven for a few minutes. A loving and toasty way to say "I love you!"

Send the cards out as soon as you can. If they're not finished yet, hire the neighborhood elves to expedite addressing so he won't have to.

Bake a real old-fashioned gingerbread house to surprise him and put a sprig of holly on the door.

Set his shoes out for St. Nicholas' arrival and remind St. Nick to fill them up.

Tie green velvet bows in your hair before bed.

Leave an extra half hour to freshen up and relax a bit before he gets home to face the after-shopping you.

Go together to look for The Tree before the crowd zeroes in on the forest.

When he's coming down with the flu, fix him a glass of warm milk at bedtime and soothe him to sleep with a lullaby.

Ask him to thumb through the slew of Christmas cookie recipes and pick out his favorites. *All* his favorites.

Make him a baby-block paperweight out of wood and inscribe it "I Love You."

Start doing pre-ski exercises now and get him involved, too.

Put a little July into December by taking a jaunt down to the local indoor swimming pool.

Holiday-up the dinner salad by making a wreath out of parsley and adding lots of cherry tomatoes for ornaments. Heap cucumbers, shrimp, cottage cheese, and radishes in the middle. Accent with a red velvet bow.

Make love in front of the Christmas tree by the light of its lights.

Clean out the fireplace and spruce it up early so Santa won't have to.

On Forefathers Day invite all the grandparents over to help trim the tree. Request them to bring something from their own childhood trees.

Call him at the office to tell him you love him more in December than you did in May.

After his steaming shower, dry him off and tell him that real sauna-takers run out into the snow naked next, but cool sheets will do.

Let him wake up in the morning to find you in his arms.

Break out the peaches in wine that you made last summer. You did, didn't you?

Hang some mistletoe all over the house. And don't let him ignore it.

Coax a neighbor to take the other members of the household out to a movie so you two can try out the new sleeping bag.

Just sit by the fireside holding hands and don't answer the phone.

It's Christmas Day! Make merry and glad and toast the joyous day.

Celebrate Boxing Day with an olde English tea, complete with marmalade and crumpets. It falls on the day after Christmas, and the custom was to give boxes of food and gifts to the butcher and baker and candlestick maker. Nowadays we have our own special people to give to, so today's the day.

Take charge of all the thank-you notes and don't make a big deal out of it.

Surprise him with one last tiny package kept back from under the tree.

Go sleigh riding; make snow angels; build a snowman. In other words, do all that snow stuff you haven't done since you were a kid.

Hold a huge early New Year's Eve bash tonight for all the gang. Tell them you have other plans for tomorrow night.

Greet the New Year together in bed with a split of champagne. It's really the very best place for you two to be.